Dear Parents and Educators,

Welcome to Penguin Young Readers! As parents and educators, you know that each child develops at his or her own pace—in terms of speech, critical thinking, and, of course, reading. Penguin Young Readers recognizes this fact. As a result, each Penguin Young Readers book is assigned a traditional easy-to-read level (1–4) as well as a Guided Reading Level (A–P). Both of these systems will help you choose the right book for your child. Please refer to the back of each book for specific leveling information. Penguin Young Readers features esteemed authors and illustrators, stories about favorite characters, fascinating nonfiction, and more!

No Bones!

LEVEL **4**

GUIDED
READING
LEVEL **N**

This book is perfect for a **Fluent Reader** who:
• can read the text quickly with minimal effort;
• has good comprehension skills;
• can self-correct (can recognize when something doesn't sound right); and
• can read aloud smoothly and with expression.

Here are some **activities** you can do during and after reading this book:
• Descriptive Words: A descriptive word is one that points out a specific characteristic of someone or something. The author of this book uses a lot of descriptive words to show us what animals without bones look like. For example, octopuses have "big" brains and sea slugs are "sneaky." Reread the story, pointing out any descriptive words that you see.
• Using a Glossary: A glossary, like a dictionary, tells you what words mean. Look at the words and their definitions in the glossary at the back of this book. Then write an original sentence for each word.

Remember, sharing the love of reading with a child is the best gift you can give!

—Sarah Fabiny, Editorial Director
  Penguin Young Readers program

*Penguin Young Readers are leveled by independent reviewers applying the standards developed by Irene Fountas and Gay Su Pinnell in *Matching Books to Readers: Using Leveled Books in Guided Reading*, Heinemann, 1999.

PENGUIN YOUNG READERS
An Imprint of Penguin Random House LLC

Smithsonian

This trademark is owned by the Smithsonian Institution and is registered
in the U.S. Patent and Trademark Office.

Smithsonian Enterprises:
Christopher Liedel, President
Carol LeBlanc, Senior Vice President, Education and Consumer Products
Brigid Ferraro, Vice President, Education and Consumer Products
Ellen Nanney, Licensing Manager
Kealy Gordon, Product Development Manager

Smithsonian National Museum of Natural History
Karen Osborn, Research Zoologist/Curator, Department of Invertebrate Zoology

Photo credits: cover: © iStock/aurigadesign; flap: © iStock/snpolus; page 3: © iStock/LauraDin;
pages 4–5: © iStock/richcarey; page 6: © iStock/GoodOlga; page 7: © Thinkstock/moodboard;
page 9: NOAA/CBNMS, photographer: Rick Starr; page 10: © iStock/OceanBodhi; page 11: © iStock/
AndamanSE; page 12: dkimages/Frank Greenaway; page 13 © iStock/atese; page 14: © iStock/
mychadre77; page 15: (top) © iStock/PamSchodt; page 15: (bottom) NOAA Okeanos Explorer
Program, INDEX-SATAL 2010; page 16: © iStock/Osluz; page 17: © iStock/johnandersonphoto;
pages 18–19: © iStock/CameraAngle; page 20: © iStock/WhitcombeRD; page 21: © iStock/g-miner;
page 23: © iStock/Howard Chew; page 24: © iStock/kavram; page 25: © iStock/joci03; page 26: (top)
NOAA Okeanos Explorer Program, Gulf of Mexico 2012 Expedition; pages 26–27 (bottom) Hidden
Ocean Expedition 2005/NOAA/OAR/OER, photographer: Kevin Raskoff, Cal State Monterey;
page 27: (top) Smithsonian National Museum of Natural History; page 28: © iStock/scubaluna;
page 29: © iStock/WhitcombeRD; page 29: (inset) Smithsonian National Museum of Natural History;
page 30: © iStock/mariusz_prusaczyk; page 31: (top) © iStock/WhitcombeRD, (bottom) Bonaire 2008:
Exploring Coral Reef Sustainability with New Technologies, NOAA/OAR/OER; page 32: © iStock/
stillwords; page 33: (top) © iStock/pilipenkoD, (bottom) © Thinkstock/Purestock; page 34: (top)
© iStock/_jure, (bottom) © Nilanjan Bhattacharya/Hemera; pages 36–37: © iStock/klaus-bodo;
pages 38–39: © iStock/IMPALASTOCK; page 39: (inset) © LAByrne; page 40: Major Ashleigh Smythe,
Ph.D., Virginia Military Institute; page 41: Lophelia II 2008: Deepwater Coral Expedition: Reefs, Rigs,
and Wreck, NOAA; page 42: © Casey Dunn; page 43: © iStock/atese; page 44: © iStock/para827;
page 45: NOAA Okeanos Explorer Program, Océano Profundo 2015: Exploring Puerto Rico's
Seamounts, Trenches, and Troughs; page 46: © Stockbyte/Comstock Images; page 47: © iStock/
Damlow; page 48: © iStock/Dennis Burns.

PENGUIN YOUNG READERS

LEVEL
4
FLUENT
READER

☀ Smithsonian
NO BONES!

by Karen Romano Young

Penguin Young Readers
An Imprint of Penguin Random House

Contents

Bones or No Bones?

vertebrate

vertebrate

invertebrate

Vertebrates are animals that have
backbones, or spines, inside. A spine
helps support an animal's body.
It gives it shape and helps it move.

Most of the animals in the world *don't* have backbones. They are **invertebrates**. There are more than a million **species** of invertebrates. Most of them live in the ocean.

invertebrate

vertebrate

No skeleton? No problem.

Marine invertebrates like octopuses, sea stars, jellies, worms, and crabs have their own ways of getting around, getting food—and not getting eaten!

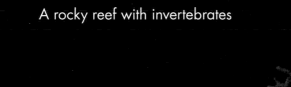

A rocky reef with invertebrates

9

Mollusks on the Move

A **mollusk** is an invertebrate with a soft body. Octopuses, squid, clams, oysters, and mussels are all mollusks. But they're not all the same!

Octopuses have big brains and eight long arms with suckers. They can squeeze into tight spots to hide. Or they can use their suckers to hold on to things and then scoot away.

Octopus escape!

Octopus sucker

A squid uses ink.

If an enemy like a shark swims near . . . *whoosh*! The squid shoots out a cloud of dark ink and is gone!

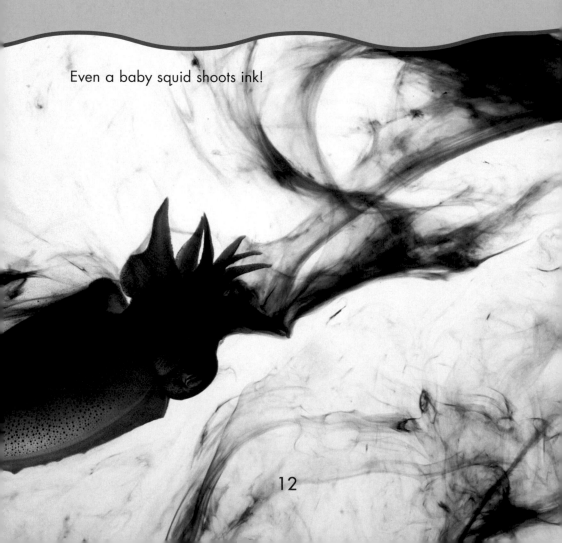

Even a baby squid shoots ink!

Speedy squid take off faster than the fastest human runner.

Clams, oysters, and mussels are mollusks in shells. They each have a double shell with a hinge like a door. The shell opens to let in water full of food. The soft body inside **filters** the food out of the water.

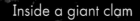

Inside a giant clam

An oyster bed

The clamshell's hinge

A sea snail is safe inside its shell.

Mollusks like snails and whelks have one hard shell. They can pull up inside it for protection.

They also each have a mouth
and a foot! With this strong
foot, they can grip food and
then eat it.

Sea slugs are sneaky mollusks that don't want to be a snack! They use **camouflage** to hide from **predators**.

Their colors help sea slugs blend in with the background. Enemies don't spot these marine invertebrates in the sand, coral, or sponge.

Sting and Shine

Coral are marine invertebrates. Coral can live and grow together and form a crusty **reef**.

All kinds of marine life find food, homes, even hideouts in coral reefs.

Do you see the fish hiding in this coral?

Some anemones live—and *eat*—among the coral. They wave their **tentacles** and blink like lights. This attracts fish.

When a fish floats close enough, the anemone zaps it with poison darts.

Jellies are swimming food traps. They're found up near the surface of the sea and down in its dark deep.

A jelly also stings its prey with poison darts. Then it pulls the prey into its mouth and belly, which are under the jelly's bell.

If you're a predator, watch out. That sting can zing you!

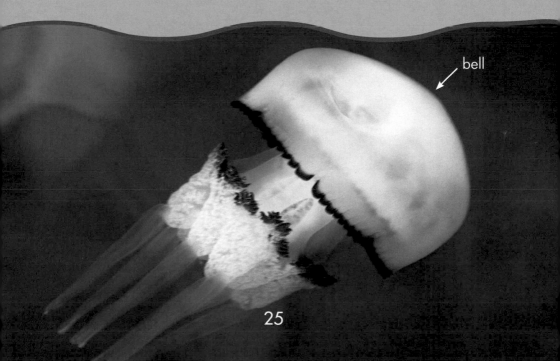

bell

A siphonophore sweeps along in the
deep ocean like a swimming mop. It's a
big **colony** of jellies that live together as
if they were one animal.

A siphonophore sparkles in the dark.

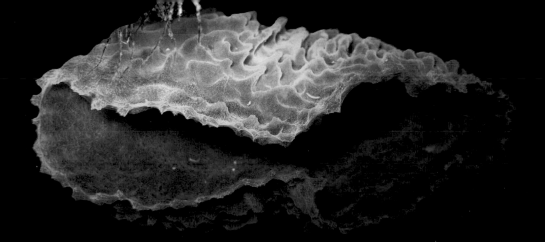

Many marine invertebrates can light their bodies like this. It's called **bioluminescence** (say: bi-oh-loo-min-ES-entz).

Lighting up in the dark sea sends a message. It could mean the animal is looking for a mate—or a meal!

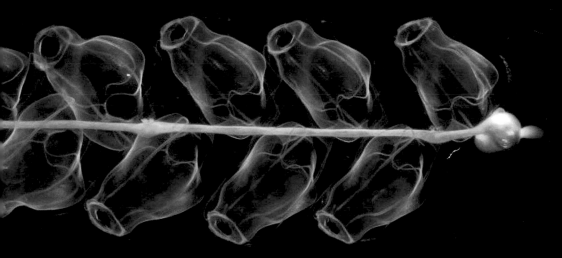

These Sponges
Aren't Square

There are thousands of sponge species in the ocean.

Sponges have no bones. But they do have shapes like tubes, curls, barrels, fans, or branches.

Sponges can be tiny or towering. They can even glow in colors.

Sponges may not look alive, but they're animals! (Some sponges people use are really dead, dry sea sponges.)

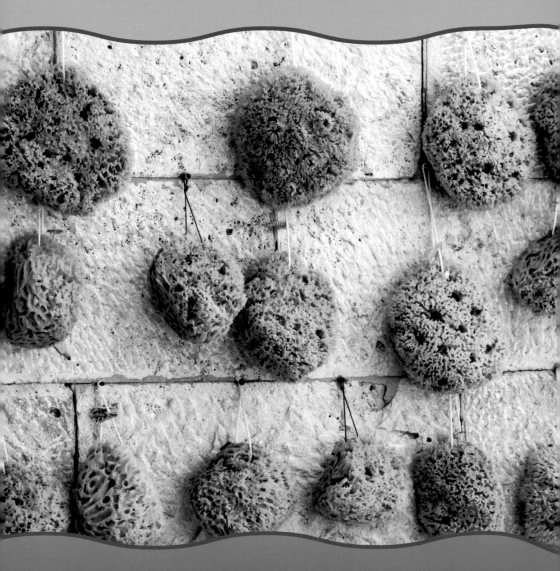

Young sponges attach themselves to rocks or reefs. Sometimes fish and crabs wriggle into a sponge and find shelter there.

Bones on the Outside

Lobsters, crabs, shrimps, and krills are **crustaceans** (say: kru-STAY-shuns). They have skeletons on the outside to protect their soft insides.

Crab

Krill

Lobster

33

As they grow, crustaceans **molt**, or shed their skeletons. For safety, lobsters hide in rock caves when they molt. They grow a new outer skeleton soon, but it won't be red.

Lobsters are blue, green, or brown in the ocean. They only turn red when you cook them.

Like some other invertebrates, shrimps start off as eggs. They hatch at the surface of the sea. As they grow, their bodies change.

They have powerful eyes to help them spot food.

This species of marine invertebrate is older than the dinosaurs!

The horseshoe crab may look scary, but it's harmless. It uses its long pointed tail for steering or to flip itself up if a wave knocks it over.

Wiggly Worms

Worms have no bones. The ocean has plenty of these invertebrates.

Marine roundworms are so tiny you need a microscope to see them. They mostly live inside other animals.

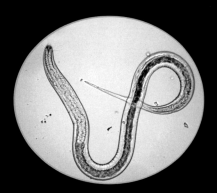

Marine roundworm

Giant tubeworms live in deep parts of the ocean that have no light. You'd have to be in a submarine to see them.

Tubeworms

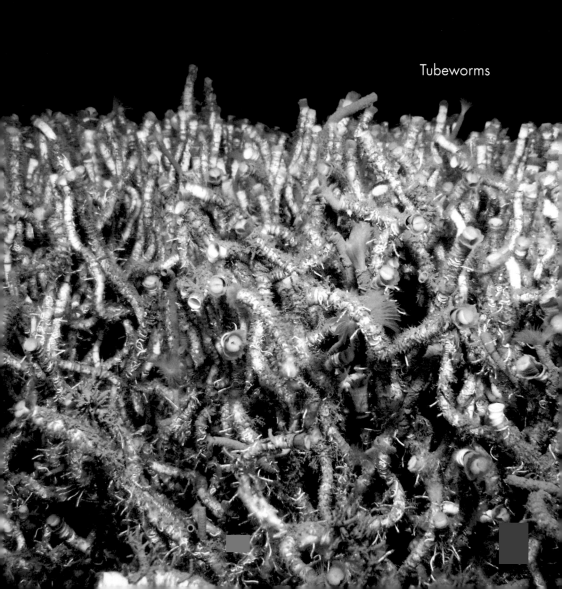

The bodies of **bristle** worms are lined with hard, stiff hairs. They use these bristles to swim or dig.

Most bristle worms light up to attract prey. Others use lights so *they* don't become prey.

These bristle worms throw off light "bombs." Fish dive and attack the bombs—and the bristle worms get away!

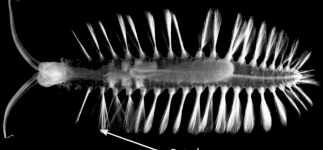

Bristle

Some worms in the sea are flatworms. You might see one on a coral reef if you go scuba diving.

Flatworms shaped like ribbons ripple through the water.

More Boneless Bodies

Animal? Vegetable? Invertebrate!
Other boneless bodies in the ocean
include sea cucumbers.

A sea pig is a kind of sea cucumber.
It's pink and has ten to fourteen stubby
"legs." Sea pigs like to eat in a group.

This marine invertebrate has no spine, but lots of spikes. The sea urchin has spikes and ribs all around its body. It's protected from danger on all sides.

But that doesn't stop another invertebrate: the sea star.

A sea star pushes its stomach through its mouth, inside out. Then it pulls it back in, food and all.

If a sea star loses a **limb**, it can regrow one. Scientists are trying to understand how. What they learn may help people grow new arms and legs, too.

Make no bones about it! Invertebrates are amazing!

Glossary

bioluminescence: the ability to light up one's body

bristle: a stiff body hair

camouflage: coloring or structure that makes something look like its surroundings

colony: a group of animals that live together as one

crustaceans: animals with skeletons on the outside of their bodies, two antennae, and jointed legs

filters: removes something not wanted or keeps something wanted

invertebrates: animals without backbones

limbs: arms and legs

marine: having to do with the ocean

mollusks: the group of animals with boneless soft bodies that includes snails, slugs, octopuses, and other animals

molt: to lose a body covering and replace it with a new one

predator: an animal that hunts other animals for food

reef: a line of rocks or coral in the ocean

species: a group of animals or plants that are similar and can produce young animals or plants

tentacles: an animal's long arms

vertebrates: animals with backbones